THE BEGINNER'S GUIDE TO KINDLE OASIS 3 (10TH GENERATION)

The Complete Guide to Setup and Manage Your e-Reader. Includes Troubleshooting Tips and Tricks

Tech Reviewer

@2019 copyright

TABLE OF CONTENT

How to Use this Book

Welcome! Thank you for purchasing this book and trusting us to lead you right in operating your new device. This book has covered every detail and tips you need to know about the Kindle Oasis 3 to get the best from the device.

To better understand how the book is structured, I would advise you read from page to page after which you can then navigate to particular sections as well as make reference to a topic individually. This book has been written in the simplest form to ensure that every user understands and gets the best out of this book. The table of content is also well outlined to make it easy for you to reference topics as needed at the speed of light.

Thank you.

Other Books by Tech Reviewer

- Fire TV Stick; 2019 Complete User Guide to Master the Fire Stick, Install Kodi and Over 100 Tips and Tricks https://amzn.to/2FnmcQ9

- Amazon Echo Dot 3rd Generation: Advanced User Guide to Master Your Device with Instructions, Tips and Tricks https://amzn.to/31PaBTF

- Mastering Your iPhone X: iPhone X User Guide for Beginners and Seniors (2019 Version) https://amzn.to/2JiywGW

- Amazon Echo Dot 3rd Generation: Advanced User Guide to Master Your Device with Instructions, Tips and Tricks https://amzn.to/31PaBTF

- Mastering your iPhone XR: iPhone XR User Guide for Beginners, New iPhone XR Users and Seniors https://amzn.to/31V4YU1

- Mastering Your iPhone XS: iPhone XS User Guide for Beginners, Seniors and New iPhone XS Users https://amzn.to/2XizMzm

Introduction

The Kindle Oasis 3 10th generation happens to be the most current member of the Amazon Kindle e-reader family.

This amazing e-reader which comes with warm light feature as well as a free 6 months Kindle unlimited subscription was launched by Amazon on July 24, 2019. It can be called the best model from the company so far. Its major selling point is that it comes with a color temperature system that adds orange LED lights to help with the front-lit display.

This new kindle device is the first of its kind to have an adjustable warm light. You can set the color temperature of the front light to go warm. This is very helpful if you read a lot in the evening as the blue light, which is perfect for day time reading, can cause you problems with sleeping at night. Not only can you adjust the intensity of the warm light, you can also schedule how you would like it to work during the day.

Another new addition to this device is the possibility of new owners to enjoy a 6 months limited offer of free Kindle Unlimited e-book subscription. After this free offer, you can automatically renew for $9.99 monthly.

The device has its own covers designed by Amazon which is sold separately from the device. You have three variants to select from: Leather cover, water-safe fabric cover or protective premium leather cover.

Waterproof

Do not worry if your device falls into water or liquid as the device comes with IPX8 waterproof rating and can withstand being immersed in 2 meters of fresh water for up to 60 minutes. However, its advisable to take out the device from the water quickly and drain to avoid damaging the device. At the later part of this book, I have included exact things you need to do if your device falls into water.

Battery Life

One single charge of the device can stay up to six weeks if your light setting is at 13 and a half-hour of daily reading with the Bluetooth and wireless deactivated. The device charges fast and gets full under 3 hours if charging with an Amazon 5W charger (not included in the box) or from a computer USB. The battery life consumes faster when connected to the internet with Bluetooth on, based on this, I would advise that you disable Wi-fi and Bluetooth when not in use.

Audiobooks

The new Oasis 3 comes with audiobook functionality, this means that you can buy an audiobook section from the Amazon bookstore. To do this, simply visit the Kindle store, there you would see two tabs, one for e-books and one for Audiobooks. Click on either of the tabs to take you to the exact section in the kindle store.

You can pair your device with Bluetooth-enabled speakers or headphones to use the audiobook service. There is no headphone jack on this device and so, you would need the Bluetooth enabled headphones if you like to use the audiobook features.

Kindle Oasis 3 Spec

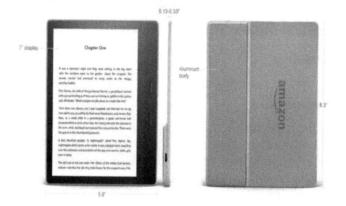

- Waterproof
- Screen resolution: 1680 × 1264 pixels
- Adjustable warm light
- 16 levels of grayscale
- Screen: 7-inch E-Ink Carta touchscreen
- 25 front light LEDs
- 300 PPI Pixel density

- No MicroSD card
- Colors: Champagne gold and graphite
- Weight: 6.6 oz / 188 g
- Storage capacity: 8GB, 32GB
- Dimensions   6.3 × 5.6 × 0.13-0.33 in / 159 × 141 × 3.4-8.4 mm
- Free cloud storage for all Amazon content
- Wi-fi connectivity: can be connected to both private and public Wi-Fi networks or hotspots.
- Warranty: Comes with a 1-year limited warranty and service included.

Price

The cost of the new e-reader is the same as the previous models. For the 8GB internal memory variant with special offers, the price is set at $249.99 while the 32GB variant with special offers costs $279.99. Please find below a complete quote on the prices

- 8 GB, Wi-Fi, with special offers – $249.99
- 8 GB, Wi-Fi, without special offers – $269.99
- 32 GB, Wi-Fi, with special offers – $279.99
- 32 GB, Wi-Fi, without special offers – $299.99
- 32 GB, Wi-Fi + Cellular, without special offers – planned

This book is a complete user guide about the Kindle Oasis 3 e-reader. Here, you would learn the complete steps for every configuration, helpful tips for troubleshooting and quick fixes and so much more.

Chapter 1: Getting Started

What is in the Box?

- The device itself.
- A quick guide.
- A USB 2.0 charging cable.

Setting Up

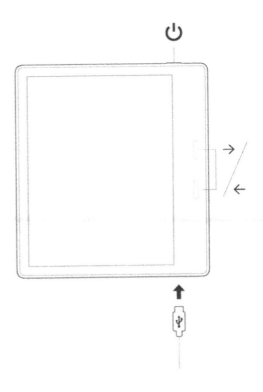

- Put on the device by pressing the power button. The power button is located at the top right of the device.
- Choose the language you prefer for the device from the drop-down list.
- Connect your device to your home Wi-fi network.
- Sign in to your Amazon account to register the device on Amazon. If you bought your device from your Amazon account, you would not need to do this step as it is automatically linked to your Amazon account.

List of Screen Icons

At the top part of your device on the home screen, you would see icons that tell you about the status of your device. If you want to view these icons while reading a book, simply tab the top of the screen for the icons to display.

- **Wi-Fi icon** 📶 : whenever you are connected to Wi-fi, you would see this icon as a notification. The more the bars, the stronger your connection.

- **Cellular Connection** 📶: this shows that your device is connected to the internet via the cellular network. The more bars you see, the stronger your connection.

- **Airplane Mode icon** ✈: this is a notification that flight mode is activated. Once this icon is active, both wireless and Bluetooth goes off.

- **Bluetooth Indicator** ᛒ: This icon comes up when your device is paired to a Bluetooth device or when your device is in a pairing mode.

- **Volume Indicator** 🔊: this shows that a VoiceView screen reader or Bluetooth audio device is connected or playing.

- **Battery Icon** 🔋 : this icon shows the percentage level of the battery. When the device is charging, you would notice a lightning bolt appear on the battery icon.

- **Parental Control icon** 🔒: this icon is an indicator that parental control is active, either because you activated it or because an Amazon FreeTime profile is active.

How to Charge your Device

- Plug the USB cable to the charging port at the bottom edge of the device and attach the other end of the cable to a computer.

- If you want to use a direct power outlet, purchase the Amazon 5W power adapter for the cable. This is faster.

How to Register/ Deregister Kindle Device

- Go to the toolbar
- Click on the **Quick Action Icon**
- Then select **All Settings**
- Click on **Your Account** from the Setting page
- The system would prompt for a passcode if you enabled Sign-in approval
- After you input the passcode, a security code would be sent to your registered phone number. Input the code.
- Setup is done.

How to Switch Off/On your Device

- Tap the power button at the top edge of the device to switch on the device.
- To switch off, tap and hold the power button for a few seconds till a display of

screen options pops up, then press "**screen off**".

How to Sleep and Wake your Device

- Press the power button once to put your device to sleep.
- Repeat the same routine to wake your device.

How to Connect your Kindle Device to your Home Network

You have two options to follow when you want to connect your device to your Home network. Either the manual connection or WPS connection.

Manual Connection

- Go to "**All Settings**".
- Select "**Wi-fi and Bluetooth**" then "**Wi-fi networks**".

- Networks will display, if you do not see your home network, refresh the list to scan afresh for available networks.
- Select your home network.
- Input the password if the network is locked.
- Depending on your preference, you can either save your password for use later or not save it by opting not to save the password when providing it.
- Hit the "**Connect**" button to connect to the network.

WPS Connection

- This process is almost identical to the manual connection but a few steps make the difference.
- After carrying out the first to the fourth step in the manual connection process, press WPS on your router.

- Carry out the fifth and the sixth step in the manual process, then hit the WPS button to connect to your home network.

Tips on your Network Connectivity

- Check your router for the default password if you can't remember your network password.
- Switch on and off the airplane mode via quick action on the toolbar to rectify connectivity issues.
- Reach out to your internet service provider or your network administrator if you still have issues connecting.

How to Turn on VoiceView During Device Setup

With the VoiceView screen reader, you are able to navigate your Kindle device using special gestures, listen to over millions of books and get voice guidance when you interact with on-screen items. You can use this feature to pair a Bluetooth audio device when setting up your device. To activate the VoiceView, follow the steps below:

- Press the Power button once for your device to come on.
- Wait for approximately 45 seconds.
- Set your Bluetooth audio device ready for pairing.
- Press the power button and hold for 9 seconds.
- Place two fingers on the screen for a second, ensure to space the fingers, remove the fingers after a second then wait for about 2 minutes until you hear an audio sound.
- Once you hear the audio on your Bluetooth device, place your two fingers spaced on the screen

- Once the audio device is connected to the Bluetooth device and the VoiceView is enabled for the first time, the screen would pop up the VoiceView tutorial.
- The system would prompt you to complete setup which includes connecting to a wireless network and registering your device.

Troubleshooting Tips

If no audio sound comes from your Bluetooth device within 2 minutes of ending the 5th step, check that the Bluetooth device is in a pairing mode then repeat the 4th and 5th step.

How to Turn on VoiceView after Device Setup

- Be sure that the Bluetooth audio device is on then wake your kindle device by pressing on the power button

- Press down the power button for about 9 seconds
- Next, place your two fingers spaced on the screen.
- VoiceView audio will begin after six seconds

How to Manage VoiceView Settings

- Click on Quick action icon on your toolbar
- Select **All Settings**
- Click on **Accessibility** from the Settings page
- If the VoiceView option is currently active, you would see **VoiceView Settings** rather than **All Settings** option

Chapter 2: Operating your Kindle Device

The Kindle Oasis comes with a touchscreen interface that makes it easy for you to carry out several task by just tapping the screen or swiping your finger. Simply tap on an item to select it. For example, tap the menu icon on the cover of an item to view the options available.

Your Device Home Screen

The Home screen has three sections: "Reading Lists", "Recommended for You" and "Recently Accessed Items".

- **Recently Accessed Items:** this is at the left side of your interface, it shows your first, second and third most recently accessed contents. For books, it shows the reading progress in percentage on the book cover. If you want to view more of your library, click on "**Your Library**" link.

- **Reading Lists:** at the right side of your home screen, you would see your Kindle books, free samples as well as Audiobooks that you added to your **'Goodreads Want to Read'** and **'Amazon Lists'** shelf.

- **Recommended for You:** at the bottom of the first page of your Home screen, you would see the recommended books, books from your Goodreads friends, Kindle tips and lots more. You can scroll, swipe or tap to view more.

- To locate your library, go to the upper left of your screen.

The Toolbar Icons

The buttons under the toolbar are explained below along with how to activate or deactivate.

- **Home:** on the home interface, you can access a number of contents stored on your Kindle device.

- **Back:** tap this to go back to where you were. For instance, you click an in-text link while reading a book, you click "back" to go back to your current line in that book to continue reading.

- **Quick actions:** this icon houses certain features such as "Screen light", "Warmth Controls", "Bluetooth", "Sync my Kindle", "Airplane Mode" and "All settings". This last feature (All settings) doesn't show when the VoiceView feature is active. The "VoiceView" feature shows instead.

- **Screen light:** You use this setting to decrease or increase the light of your device screen by either a sliding gesture or clicking the + and – sign for a more precise setting.

- **Warmth:** this setting works on its own if auto-brightness is activated. But manually, you can raise or lower the warmth between cool white and white amber by either the sliding gesture or tapping the + and – sign.
- **Bluetooth:** This feature activates or deactivates your Bluetooth connection.
- **Sync my Kindle:** this feature syncs your device with Kindle reading apps and other supported devices owned by you.
- **All settings:** this setting helps the user to personalize his kindle experience.
- **Goodreads:** this feature can be accessed by signing in (if you already have an account) or signing up (new user).
- **Store:** this feature gives you access to the Kindle and the Audible store (the Audible store is restricted to some countries). This feature works with a network connection.

- **Search:** touch inside the search box to execute your search. If you want to exit, touch the area outside the search box.

- While reading a book, the menu will display options such as "**Settings**", "**Shop Audible Store**", "**Shop Kindle Store**", "**Vocabulary Builder**", "**Word Wise**", "**About this Book**", "**About the Author**" (this displays only for books that have the author profile), "**sync to furthest page read**", "**X-ray**" and "**Share**".

- **Page display:** this setting enables the user to configure reading settings for his page display. "Font size" and "line spacing" are some of the options in this setting.

- **Go To:** this shows the title of your book, the chapters, how the book began and what it contains. Use the page option if you want to scroll further. Touch the

"**Notes tab**" icon if you want to have access to your notes and highlights. **Bookmarks:** click to create new bookmarks or remove existing bookmarks on the current page. You can also view bookmarks that were created previously. When you click your bookmark, a preview will display, click it to go to the precise location, tap outside to exit this feature.

Chapter 3: Navigating Settings

In this chapter, we would discuss how to customize your Device Settings.

To go to your Settings,

- Click on the **Quick Action** icon on the toolbar
- Then click on **All Settings**

OR

- Click on the menu icon then select "**Settings**"

You would not be able to access the Settings option if your device is not registered to an Amazon account.

You would see several categories under settings. These include Your Account, Wi-Fi & Bluetooth, Household & Family Library, Language & Dictionaries, Reading Options, Device Options, Parental Controls, Accessibility and Contact Us.

I would now explain each of the menus under different categories:

Your Account

Under this category, you have;

- **The device name**: this setting is to configure the name on display at the top left corner of your home screen.
- **Personal Information:** here, you can add personal and contact information on the device that can help to identify your device if it gets stolen or misplaced. Information such as your residential address, mobile number, etc.
- **Social networks**: you can use this setting to sync your device with your social media accounts. This is helpful for times you wish to share contents with your online friends.
- **Deregister device:** this setting is for deactivating your device, wiping its

contents and cutting it off from your Amazon account. When this occurs, many features linked to your account will cease to function on the device, however, items you bought from the Amazon store would still be available in the cloud and you can access them at any time. After deregistering the device, you can link another Amazon account to the device.

- **Special offers:** this setting is limited to Kindle devices with this particular feature. Helps you to manage how the special offers are shown on your device.

- **Send-to-Kindle email:** this setting helps the user to input the mail address, through which he can get his documents on his kindle device. Such documents are converted to Kindle format and may incur charges.

Household and Family Library

With this setting, you can add individuals to your household for the purpose of sharing content.

Wi-Fi and Bluetooth

- **Airplane mode:** If activated, this feature cuts off network connection to the device.
- **Wi-fi networks:** this feature displays networks you can connect to and it also shows the network you are already connected to.
- **Delete Passwords:** to erase passwords saved to your Amazon account from the device.
- **Bluetooth:** Switch on or off Bluetooth
- **Bluetooth Devices:** this feature helps you take out, add new Bluetooth devices

as well as see the list of available devices. It can be used to connect to devices like speakers and headphones.

Device Options

- **Device info:** this setting displays some technical details about the device. Click the "**What's New**" button to verify if your Kindle is updated or not.

- **Display Size:** to personalize the layout of your page and preferences pertaining to display. For instance, you can opt for the normal or a larger font size depending on what suits you. However, larger font size will not display all the contents of some pages. Amazon free time, store, vocabulary builder and search are areas the large font size won't apply.

- **Device Password:** here, you are able to restrict access to your device by creating a passcode. After this is set, you will need to input the code each time you wake, restart or switch on the device. If you can't remember your code, you would need to contact the customer service.

- **Device time:** to set the time displayed at the top right of the screen.

- **Restart:** you can reboot your device by either holding the power button till the power options pop up and you select restart or you reboot by holding the power button till the light on the body of the device turns amber and flashes four times, then you release the power button.

- **Reset:** This option will take your device back to its default setting as if it were a new device. It will also wipe all the saved contents on the device. However, the contents can be retrieved from the cloud. Proceed to reset only if told to do so by the customer service. Also, remember to back up contents you do not want to lose before resetting. When the device restarts, you would need to register again and download your contents from the cloud. You would also need to set a new passcode if you would like your system to be passcode protected.

- **Advanced options:** to activate "Whispersync" for books, manage storage and privacy. It is also used to update the device if there are available updates as well as to set options for the home and library and to delete or archive contents.

- **Home and Library:**

Under the Home and Library menu, you have the **Home Screen View** to select if you would like to hide or display Kindle store recommended contents as well as to disable or enable reading lists.

Audible Content: from this option, you can select the option for your Audible books to show in both the Library and Home or for the cloud Audible items to show in the "Audible" filter in the library. All Audible items you download would still show in Home screen.

Update Your Kindle: this is where you get to update your software to the latest version. If there are no available updates, this menu would be greyed.

Whispersync for books: Disable or enable the automatic backup of your most recent page reads, annotations, collections, and furthest page read to the Amazon's servers.

Reading Options

- **Page refresh:** to set your device to refresh your screen each time you turn the page.

- **Next in series:** to show an option to purchase the next book on series when rounding up the current book.

- **Nightlight:** can be activated to lower the brightness level while reading at night.

- **Language learning:** to enable or disable vocabulary builder and word wise preferences.

Wordwise: when this option is enabled, your screen would pop up hints above any challenging words in several common English-language titles. Disable the "**Show Multiple-Choice Hints**" if you want to turn off various hints for a word. From the language option, select between Simplified Chinese and English Word Wise hints.

Vocabulary Builder: Move the switch to the right or to the left to enable or disable. When this is active, every word that you look up is added to the Vocabulary Builder.

Pinyin: this would show you pronunciation guide at the top of Chinese characters.

Highlights and About the Book: to control and configure highlight preferences. Contains settings such as "highlights menu", "popular highlights", "about the book" and "book mentions".

Language and Dictionaries

- Language: This setting displays the current language for alerts, menus and dialog box and allows you to change the language to another depending on your preference.

- **Keyboards:** to enable keyboards for different language. If you have many keyboards, you would see a Globe key added to your keyboard. To select from the several keyboards, click on the globe key.

- **Dictionaries:** to set the main dictionary for each language you select.

Accessibility

- **VoiceView Screen reader:** Under this option, you can move the switch to enable or disable the VoiceView feature. With the VoiceView feature, you are able to navigate through your device with special gestures, receive audio guidance when interacting with on-screen items and also listen to several books of your choice. Under this feature you have some sub-features which are:

Tutorials: this shows you how to use the VoiceView feature with other features on the device. You can leave the tutorial by clicking on the **Exit** button at the end of your screen.

Speech Rate: here, you can control the speed of spoken feedbacks from VoiceView.

Bluetooth: this option allows you to remove, add and view all available Bluetooth audio devices. You can pair your Kindle device with several Bluetooth enabled devices like speakers and headphones.

• **Display Size:** here, you can customize your display preferences and page layout. To use the default layout and font size, chose "**Standard**". To increase the size of the font for better readability, click on **Large.** This would reduce the amount of content you would see on some pages.

This large mode is unavailable in the following areas: Amazon FreeTime, Search bar, Store and Vocabulary Builder.

- **Inverts Black and White:** inverts the image, text, and colors on all the device screens. While your text would show in white color, the background would show in black color.

Parental Controls

- **Amazon free time (known as Amazon fire for children in U.K.):** this setting enables you to customize profiles for your kids on your device, choose books from the library you want to share with them, and most importantly, cutting off their access to contents or areas you don't want them to interact with. Areas such as Audible stores, the experimental internet browser and Goodreads. Options to deregister and reset are usually deactivated once this feature is activated.

- **Restrictions:** This setting can be used to shut off access to private areas (Kindle and Audible stores, Goodreads and the web browser) manually.

- **Change password:** when you activate a restriction for the first time or set the Amazon FreeTime for kids in the UK, you would be asked to create a password. Anytime you need to make changes within the Parental control menu, you would need to input this password. Peradventure, you forget this password, go to this link to reset, www.amazon.com/devicesupport or contact the customer care center.

Contact Us

- This setting requires the use of your network connection. It is the support center. You can have access to helpful information needed to fix or troubleshoot technical issues on your device. This is also used to provide feedback to the support team.

Settings Contextual Menu

From the Settings page, clicking on the 3-dot menu icon would display the options below:

- **Kindle Store:** gives you access to the Kindle store.
- **Audible Store:** gives you access to the Audible store.
- **Update your Kindle:** this setting helps install the latest updates for your device's software. It is only activated when there are updates to install on the device.
- **Restart:** for rebooting your device.
- **Reset:** for restoring your device to factory settings.

- **Device Info:** from here you would see your device serial number, firmware version, Wi-fi MAC address, and available space. It would also show you if your device was updated recently.
- **Legal information:** This feature gives you access to legal notices pertaining to your device.

Page Turn Button

If you want to go to the next page when reading a book, simply click on the top button or click on the bottom button to go to the previous page. If you wish to set the buttons to work in line with how you hold your device, follow the steps below:

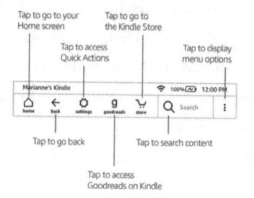

Tap to go to your Home screen
Tap to go to the Kindle Store
Tap to access Quick Actions
Tap to display menu options
Tap to go back
Tap to search content
Tap to access Goodreads on Kindle

- From the toolbar, click on the **Quick Actions** icon.
- Then click on **All Settings.**
- Next click on **Page Turn Buttons.**
- Set as preferred.

Whatever settings you have would apply even when the device is rotated. The device is programmed to go to sleep after some minutes of inactivity, then a screensaver would show on the screen.

Chapter 4

How to Get and Manage Content on your Device

Both the Audible and the Kindle stores give you a vast selection of reading contents such as Audible audiobooks, Kindle books, Kindle singles, magazines, newspapers, and blogs.

- To access the store icon, swipe down the top of the screen so the toolbar displays. Click the store icon.
- Use swiping gestures to scroll across your areas of interest in the store.
- You can search by the title of a book or category of the book or document.
- To purchase content, the store utilizes your Amazon 1-click payment procedure.

- After successfully ordering, the **'Whispernet"** service directly sends the content to your Kindle device.

- It is advisable to use Wi-fi if you want to download large files like Comics or audibles. The progress rate of the download will display beneath the title of the book on the home screen. When the content is done downloading, it shows a new banner and then you can view your new content.

- Contents are sent to your Kindle device even before they are available in hard copy.

- Whispersync links your Kindle device with reading apps and other devices registered to your Amazon account, so that book samples you purchase and download within those apps are available to you at all times. This makes it possible to listen/read some pages on your

Android, iPad or iPhone using the Kindle app. When you open same content on your Kindle device, you continue right from where you left off.

- This store gives you access to thousands of audiobooks and Kindle Books.

How to Hide Recommended Content

On your home screen, you get to see several recommended items from Kindle e-reader tips, Audible stores, fun facts and lots more. If you see a recommendation you may be interested in, simply click on it to take you to the Kindle store where you would see more details, view reviews from others who may have purchased and then make your purchase if you desire. You can hide these recommendations by following the steps below:

- Go to the Quick Actions icon on the toolbar then select "**All settings**".

- Click on "**Device options**" then select "**Advanced options**".
- Click on "**Home & Library**", then set the option "**Home Screen View**" to OFF.

How to Manage your Kindle Library

Your device is able to store audiobooks, newspapers, books, personal documents, magazines, and blogs.

- If you want to view your contents, click on "**library**" on your home screen.
- Contents that have been downloaded to your Kindle shows a mark on the lower left side of the cover image (if you are on grid view), and the lower right side (For list view).
- To access downloaded content only, click on "**downloaded**" at the upper left side of the screen.

- To modify the display outlook of your content, click on "**All items**" of the recently chosen filter, then choose list or grid view. Grid view is the default view on your device.

- To access more information on specific contents, as well as a list of options pertaining to it, click the icon (three vertical dots) on the item's cover.

- Menu options such as "**Play audible**", "**Add to Free Time Library**" (Add to Amazon Fire for Kids Library in the U.K.), "**View Bookmarks**", "**Add to Home**", "Add to Collection", " Search this Book", " Remove from Device", "Go-To", "Add to Goodreads shelf", "Share" and "View on Goodreads".

- For list view, you can also tap and hold the content's cover to view these options.

How to Sort Content in the Library

By default, the device is designed to sort your items by the most recent items down, this means that the new additions and the content you are reading currently would show at the top.

- To modify the mode of sorting, click on the current name of the sort order, which is at the right side of the screen beneath the toolbar.
- Sort options include: "Author", "Title", "Recent" and "Collection".
- Select the option you would want your items to show under.

How to Filter Content in the Library

- Click on the **filter** option on your library interface.

- Filter by "read state" is the first option and includes two sub-options: "read" and "unread".

- To access only your read content, click on "**read**". To access only your unread contents, touch "**unread**". Books that have been read are instantly marked in your library as a read item.

- Filter by "Content-type" is the second option and includes six filter options: "Books", "Collections", "Comics", "Periodicals", "Audibles" and "Docs".

- For Kindle users who have activated the "Amazon Household" and **active sharing** option, you would see two new filtering options under "**All items**": These are "Your Items" and "Shared Items".

- To access your items only, click on "Your Items". To access items shared by other individuals in the Amazon household, click on "**Shared Items**".

- Items backed up or stored in the cloud can also be filtered. To access this, click on "**All**" at the upper left of your screen.

How to Create a New Cloud Collection

With the cloud collections, you are able to organize contents of your device into customized categories that would be stored in the cloud. All devices linked to the same Amazon account and support cloud collections would have access to your collections. You are free to add as many contents as you like including personal documents and books. You can also add items to more than one collection. While you cannot add audible contents to the collections, you can, however, add the kindle book version. Follow the steps below to create a new collection:

- Go to Library from your home screen
- Click on the menu icon on your library interface.
- Tap "Create New Collection".
- Using the keyboard that will pop up, create a name for the collection then hit "OK".
- On the next screen, you would see a list of available items on your device that can be added to the collection.
- To add the items you want, tick the checkbox beside them. When you are done adding items, click "Done".
- You can subsequently add or subtract items from your collection. Just click the menu option on the content's cover and select "**Add/remove items**". You can also touch and hold the cover for the option to display.
- There are more options such as "Remove from device", "Delete" or "Rename".

- To remove the collection from your Kindle device, click the menu icon on the collection's cover or touch and hold the cover till the options display.
- To exit the collection, tap the home or back icon.
- Items once stored in the collection will go back to being displayed on your home screen, and in the cloud, once the collection is deleted.

Tips to Note*

When you delete a collection created in a reading app or device that supports cloud collections like the Kindle device, the collection would be deleted from the cloud and other devices registered to the same Amazon account.

If you delete a collection from your Kindle device, it does not automatically delete the contents of the collection from your device or even the cloud. Once a collection is deleted, all items stored in the collection would return to the Home screen and in the cloud.

How to Check Available Storage

- Click on the **Quick Actions** icon from the toolbar.
- Then click on "All settings".
- Click the menu icon then "**Device Info**".

How to Transfer Content between Devices

To be able to move contents from your old device to your new one would depend on the source of the contents. Contents that you bought from the Kindle store like periodicals, books, and magazines are automatically stored in Amazon cloud, ready for you to download whenever needed. For all your personal documents that were emailed to your device after you have enabled Personal Document Archiving are automatically saved in the cloud.

For personal documents that were moved directly to your old device but not via email would need to be transferred manually.

How to Download Content from the Cloud

- Click on the Library icon on the Home screen, at the top left side of the screen.
- Click "**All**" at the upper left side of your library screen.
- To cancel the download process, simply touch the content's title.
- Downloaded content can either be accessed from the home screen or in the library.

How to Manually Transfer Contents

Follow the steps below to move items that were not emailed to the old device from your old Kindle device to the new one.

- Attach your device to a computer using the USB cord.

- Manually move the folders/ files from the old device to the document folder of the new device.
- For large documents, create subfolders inside the document folder.
- Note that you should only put a maximum of 2,000 files per subfolder.

How to Remove Content from your Kindle

There are three ways to do this; You can do a quick archive of the contents you want to remove or you can remove them based on content type and the third option is manually removing the items one after the other. Please follow the guide below for any of your preferred choices:

Manual Removal: to take out individual items,

- Click on the Menu icon on the cover of the item in Grid view or at the right side of the screen in List view

- Then click on "**Remove from Device**."

Another way to view this option is to press and hold on a collection's cover or name. The items in the collection would still remain in the Cloud for you to download whenever you want. Personal documents are not automatically saved in the Cloud except if they were sent to your device via email and you have the Personal Document Archiving option enabled.

Any file that you sent to your device with the USB cable would be permanently deleted, as they are not saved in the Cloud.

Tip*

To change from Grid to List view, click on the currently selected filter or on "**All Items**" then select either Grid or List view.

Removal Based on Content-Type: You can choose to delete items based on the type of contents like Periodicals, Audiobooks, Books, Docs, Samples, etc. The items you downloaded from Cloud would still be available by clicking on **All** in the library while the ones transferred via USB would be permanently deleted.

Quick Archive: With this option, you can free up space by deleting downloaded items that you haven't accessed of recent. The items you downloaded from Cloud would still be available by clicking on **All** in the library while the ones transferred via USB would be permanently deleted.

Chapter 5: Reading on your Kindle Device

How to Configure your Page Refresh

You can enable your device to refresh the page whenever you turn your device to any angle. To do this, follow the steps below:

- Touch "**All settings**", go to "**Reading options**".
- Go to "**page refresh**" and configure it to your preference.
- To refresh settings for photo-oriented content such as magazines, photobook, and comics, tap the menu icon.
- Toggle the page refresh to on or off as desired.

How to Customize Textual Display

- Go to the toolbar and click on "**page display**"

- From the drop-down menu, click on **"Font and Page Setting"**. From this setting, you can customize other settings below.

- Click the **"Font"** tab to choose your preferred font from a list of available fonts.

- To configure the font size, increase or decrease using the sliding gesture or tap the + and – sign.

- A shortcut to changing your font size while viewing your content is to use your fingers to make a pinching gesture on the screen.

- To configure line spacing and size of the margin, click the "Page" tab. You can also click the option to toggle between landscape and portrait screen style. This can be done while reading your content and adjust text alignment.

- Under the Page tab, you can also change the alignment of text. Available options are left justified and justified.

- Click on the "**Reading Settings**" tab to choose the reading progress tracker you prefer, and choose if you want your clock to be hidden or displayed while reading.

- To save your current settings for a page, font and reading options to a new page display theme that will be added as an option in the page display menu, click on the "**theme tab**".

- You can also use the theme tab to delete, manage visibility and rename reading themes on the "page display" menu.

How to Modify your Default Dictionary

- Click on the **Quick Action** icon on the toolbar whether from the home screen or when reading.

- Then click on "**All settings**"

- Click on "**Language and Dictionaries**".

- Click on "**Dictionaries**".

- The existing dictionary would show under the dictionary language.

- An arrow at the right of language means that there are several dictionary options available for that language.

- Click on the radio button to choose your preferred dictionary then hit "OK".

- If you come across a challenging word while reading, simply touch and hold to highlight the word you want to look up in the dictionary. A card would pop-up on the screen with a definition of your selected word.

How to Turn Off Highlights

- Click on the **Quick Action** icon on the toolbar.

- Then click on "**All settings**"
- Go to "Reading Options, Highlights and About this Book".
- Disable the "Popular Highlights" feature.

How to Manage Whispersync for Book Configurations

- Click on the Quick Actions icon on the toolbar.
- Select "**All Settings**"
- Go to **Device options** from the settings page.
- Then click on "**Advanced Options**".
- Tap "**Whispersync for books**".

Chapter 6: Audio Books

How to Connect a Bluetooth Device While Opening Audiobook

- Go to the library, then tap "**downloaded**".
- Click on the audiobook you intend to listen to, an option to connect a Bluetooth device if you haven't done so will pop up.
- Enable pairing mode for your Bluetooth audio device.
- Select the Bluetooth device you intend to use.
- After a successful pairing, the audiobook will output from that device when playing. You can also access Bluetooth via settings.

How to Disable Vocabulary Builder

- Go to "**All settings**".

- Among the options you will see, select "**Vocabulary Builder**". Move the switch to the left or right to disable or enable the option.

How to Check your Child's Progress on Amazon Free Time

- Touch the profile icon beside their name, click on "**progress**".

- To access the total time used for reading, reading time per session, percentage of each read, and the number of words that were checked in the dictionary, select the "**Book Links**" at the upper left side.

- To access the number of achievements, daily goal process, books through with, minutes read, pages read and so on, select the "**Activity link**". It is located in the middle tab.

- Click the "**Achievements link**" at the upper right side to view the achievements earned by your child.

How to Add an Adult to your Amazon Household.

- Go to the **Quick Action** icon from the toolbar.
- Click on **All Settings.**
- Click on the "**Household and Family Library**" option.
- Select "**Add new person**" then "**Add adult**"
- You will be asked to hand your device to the individual you want to add to your household.
- The new user will be required to input a personal Amazon account ID and

password. If there is no existing account, please click on the displayed link to create one.

- The person will get the chance to enable sharing. They will decide if they want to share particular contents or all their purchased content with you.

- By enabling sharing, you have automatically been given permission to utilize their credit cards linked with their Amazon account to make purchases on Amazon.

- Your device will be returned to you, then you can enable sharing as well and decide if you want to share specific contents or all purchased contents. This person now has identical permission with your own credit card linked to your Amazon account.

How to Modify Features for Members of Your Household

- Go to the **Quick Action** icon from the toolbar.
- Click on **All Settings.**
- Click "**Household and Family Library**".
- Click on the desired user's name, a list of options will display.
- Options such as "**Manage family library**", "**Select devices that Show Shared content**", "**Manage Share All Books**", "**Manage Payment Methods**" and "**Remove individuals from the Household on all devices**".
- Click on the desired option and activate or disable.

Note: when one adult leave or is removed from a household, both adults would be unable to join or create a household for 180 days neither can you add another adult to the existing household for the next 180 days.

How to Find Your Send-to-Kindle Email Address

- Go to the **Quick Action** icon from the toolbar.

- Go to "**All Settings**", click on "**My Account**".

- Go to "**Send to Kindle email**", you will find the email address there.

How to Link your Device to Social Media

- Go to the **Quick Action** icon from the toolbar.

- Click on **All Settings.**

- Click "**My Account**", go to "**Social networks**".

- To do this from within your content, click on the menu icon, then select "**Share**".

- To share a part of the content, use your fingers to highlight the part you want to share. Choose the sharing option you prefer from the list that will display.

How to Utilize the Experimental Web Browser

- Click the menu icon on the home screen
- Then click on **Experimental Browser**.
- To enter a URL (Uniform Resource Locator), click on the search field at the upper section of the screen.
- Use the keyboard on the screen to type in your web address.
- To magnify a web page or image, bring two of your fingers almost joined together and then move them apart on the screen.
- To reverse this magnifying gesture, make a pinching gesture with your fingers on the screen.

- Move your fingers across the screen to scroll through the page.

- Touch hypertexts or links to access a different web page.

- To go back to the previous web page, click the back icon at the top left of the web page.

- To access previously viewed web pages, go to browser history

Chapter 7

Troubleshooting Tips/ Quick Fixes for the Kindle Oasis 10th generation

How to Fix a Frozen Screen?

If your device refuses to power on, or stops responding during use, follow the steps below:

- Press the power button and hold it for 9 seconds
- Once the power dialog box shows on the screen, click on **Restart**
- If the dialog box does not come up, hold the power button for 15 seconds until the LED light goes off

How to Fix a Slow Screen

Common causes of a slow screen include device temperature, dirty screen, pending download among other things.

- Go to menu, select **settings**.
- Hit "**menu**" under settings, click "**restart**".

What to do if you can't Register your Device

First of all, check the following;

- Check "**Your Account**" to verify that your Amazon account details are accurate. Check if you are signing with the accurate details when signing in.
- Check your device version. If the software has been upgraded to its latest version.
- Your email client isn't placing notification mails from Amazon in a junk or spam section whenever you sign in with your email.

Because Amazon requires an additional verification process for registering specific gadgets and apps. To successfully register them, follow these steps:

- opt to register your app or device.
- Sign in with your Amazon account sign in information. You will be sent a mail if you used an email address to sign in, and a text if it's a mobile number.
- Check the sent message for a one-time password which expires within a period of ten minutes.
- Repeat step 2 with the one-time password being used as your password.
- You will be notified about successful registration. If you activated two-step verification and having trouble registering devices or applications, opt for an alternative sign-in method.

What to Do if your Kindle Device is Lost or Stolen

- First of all, deregister the device from your Amazon account. This is to avoid your device being used by someone else, to make purchases on your Amazon account.
- It is advisable you note your device's serial number before deregistration.
- To deregister, launch "Manage Your Content and Device". opt for "Your Devices".
- Choose the missing device, click the "Actions" button.
- Copy the serial number of your device then contact Amazon customer care service.
- Tap "Deregister", re-tap it to round up the deregistration process.

- To reach out to the customer care service, go to the Amazon Web site, locate the help page and click "Contact Us" at the left section of the page.
- Doing this prevents your device from being registered on another Amazon account.

What to do if Content Won't Download or Sync

First of all, check the following;

- Verify that your device is connected to a wireless network. Do this by checking for the wi-fi indicator at the top just by the battery indicator.
- Check if your device is synced. If it isn't, go to settings, click "**device options**" then click "**Sync your device**".

- Check if your device is registered to the accurate Amazon account by going to "My Account". If it is the wrong account you are registered on, deregister, then register on the correct account. Check your household profiles if you are on more than one, make sure it's the correct one.

- Check your payment method, if it is working. Click on "**Your digital orders**" to check if your purchases are successful. Incomplete of failed purchases prevents the content from downloading or syncing.

- If you want to update your payment method, click "**Manage Your Content and Devices**", click settings, then click "**Digital Payment settings**".

- opt for "**edit payment method**". Make your changes there.

- Check if your Kindle's time and date are correct. Go to "**Device options**", click "**date and time**". If the automatic time zone is activated, deactivate it and go to "Time Zone" then pick your time zone.

If the issue still persists, follow these steps;

- Verify if your device supports that content you want to download or sync. For instance, if you having difficulty switching from Kindle book to the audible version, verify that the Whispersync for voice is present for that particular content.
- Deliver content through "**Manage Your Content and Devices**" by going to the tab, and then select the content you intend to deliver.
- Click on "**deliver**" then tap the content, click on deliver again.

- Touch and hold the power button until the device automatically restarts. If it doesn't restart on its own after that time frame, restart it by pressing the power button for a few seconds.

Device not Charging Properly

Follow these steps if your device doesn't stay charged or takes a much longer time to charge:

- Check your cable and power adapter (if you are using one), make sure they are well attached. Also, check if they are faulty. The cause could be either a faulty cable or adapter. Replace the faulty accessory.
- Charge your device with the recommended accessories.
- Switch off your wireless connection while charging.

- Put the device into sleep mode while charging. To do this, briefly tap the power button.
- Restart the device.
- Connect the charger to a direct power outlet.

What To Do If Your Device Is Exposed To Water

Although the Kindle device has been tested to withstand immersion in water, it is however not intended for you to use it underwater and may have some temporal effect if exposed to water. Follow the steps below if your device was dipped in water:

- First of all, remove your device from the water and strip off the cover of the device (if any).
- If your device was dipped in freshwater, detach all cables plugged to it and position the device vertically with the

charging port facing down, so the device can drain off the water.

- If it was exposed to other types of water such as saltwater, detach all cables, position the device the exact way you did in the step above, then rinse your device with fresh water. Let your charging port face the source of the water while doing that, then drain again.

- Place the device in an airy location so that it can dry thoroughly.

- Avoid drying your device using a synthetic source of heat such as an oven or microwave as this can damage your device.

- Avoid inserting a foreign material (which means anything other than the USB cable) into your USB/ charging port.

- Never intentionally expose or dip your device in any form of water or liquid generally.

Tips to Reduce Risk of Damage

- Do not intentionally dip your device in water or get it exposed to chlorinated water, saltwater, seawater or other liquids.
- Never spill food, oily substances, body cream, and other stuff on your device.
- Ensure that your device is not exposed to high-velocity water, pressurized water or very humid conditions like a steam room
- Never make your device prone to very humid conditions, fast-moving water, etc.

Care Tips

- Avoid using a cloth with a rough surface to clean your device, always use a soft cloth.

- Avoid cleaning the screen or body with abrasive substances.
- Get a cover for your device to protect it, particularly, the screen from scratches.
- Do not place your device in any place with extreme temperatures either cold or hot. A well-ventilated location with moderate sunlight is preferable.
- As much as possible, avoid using third-party accessories with your Kindle. Amazon products are preferable. If you must use an outside accessory, ensure you have gone through and understood the safety instructions that come with it.
- Contact customer service support if you want to service your device.

Battery Maintenance

- Do not for any reason, touch your battery.

- Do not expose your battery to liquid, humidity or extreme temperatures.

- Do not place foreign objects in your battery, bend, or perforate the battery.

- Avoid short-circuiting the battery and avoid exposing the battery terminals to objects that are metallic, like blades.

- Do not drop the battery or the device itself. If the battery is faulty, do not attempt to fix it. Contact customer service for that.

- Keep your device away from sources of heat while charging or during usage. Also, do not charge it near water or in very humid conditions.

- Use either the cable that came with the device to charge it or USB cables recommended for the device as well as chargers that are friendly to your device.

Tips Concerning Your Wireless Connection

- Avoid using your network connection at locations its usage is forbidden or strongly advised against. Locations such as an airplane, gas station.

- If you are in an aircraft, it is advisable you seek the permission of a flight crew member before you use your wireless connection. This is to ensure you don't cause interference with the aircraft during flight.

Other Safety Tips

- Do not fiddle your device while driving to avoid accidents on the road.

- Your device emits an electromagnetic pulse that can be dangerous to items such as credit cards because the data it contains is sourced from its magnetic chip. Avoid bringing your device close to these items.

Chapter 8: Conclusion

This user guide has all the information you need to derive the best out of your new e-reader. A good part of the content especially those for settings and troubleshooting also applies to the earlier generations of the Kindle device as there are little differences/upgrades between them and the current generation.

I recommend that you make use of the table of content to navigate through whatever options you may be interested in. You can always refer to this guide whenever you encounter any issue with using your device.

If you are pleased with the content of this book, please recommend to a friend.

Thank you.

www.ingramcontent.com/pod-product-compliance
Lightning Source LLC
Chambersburg PA
CBHW031246050326
40690CB00007B/971